ALCHEMY AND ASTRAL PROJECTION

ALCHEMY AND ASTRAL PROJECTION

ECSTATIC TRANCE IN THE HERMETIC TRADITION

KEN HENSON

FOUR CANDLES PRESS

CINCINNATI, OH

Made possible by a Curtis G. Lloyd Fellowship from the Lloyd Library and Museum

Alchemy and Astral Projection
Ken Henson
Four Candles Press

ISBN-13: 978-0615953120 (Four Candles Press)
ISBN-10: 0615953123

CONTENTS

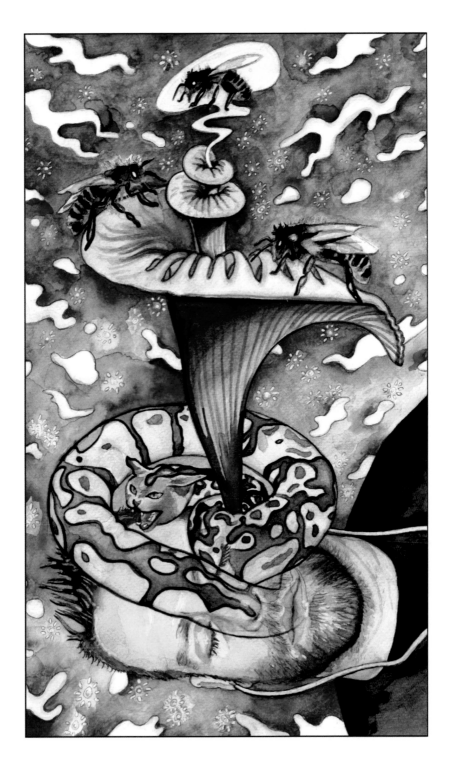

ACKNOWLEDGMENTS

> "Accordingly, a class came to believe that a projection of natural mental faculties into an advanced state of consciousness called "the wisdom faculty" constitutes the final possibility of alchemy. The attainment of this exalted condition is still believed practicable by many earnest savants. Once on this lofty plane, the individual would not be trammelled by material obstacles, but would abide in that spiritual placidity which is the exquisite realization of mortal perfection."
> -John Uri Lloyd

The quote above, from John Uri Lloyd's classic esoteric novel *Etidorhpa* (1895), is a direct link between this treatise and the institution that made it possible. *Etidorhpa*, often lumped into the sci-fi, hollow earth, and psychedelic genres, would be more accurately classified as an alchemical allegory, and not unlike Apuleius' *The Golden Ass,* a fantastical telling of initiation into the Western Mysteries Tradition.

While I have spent the better part of my life studying hermetic literature, the book you are holding is the product of a particularly intense period of study that I was afforded by a Curtis G. Lloyd Research Fellowship from The Lloyd Library and Museum. The terms of my fellowship were to read alchemy books in the Lloyd Library's magnificent collection, to write and illustrate this treatise, have an art exhibit of the paintings in this book, and give a lecture on the subject of alchemical symbolism. For these opportunities, I am deeply grateful.

I first entered the Lloyd Library and Museum in 2005 because I was aware that one of its founders, the innovative doctor of eclectic medicine, John Uri Lloyd, had written *Etidorhpa.* I wanted to inquire if the Library had in its collection any artifacts by the book's illustrator John Augustus Knapp. Most people familiar with Knapp know him as the illustrator of Manly P. Hall's classic book, *The Secret Teachings of All Ages.* It turns out that the Lloyd Library has in its archives most of the original art from *Etidorhpa,* which is very beautiful to view in person. Upon learning my interest in these topics, I was asked by Maggie and Anna Heran to give a lecture on "Knapp and the Significance of Mushrooms in Etidorhpa" to accompany an exhibit of beautiful mushroom drawings Knapp painted for John Uri's brother, the mycologist Curtis Gates Lloyd.

Thus began my descent into the rabbit hole of the history of Knapp, the Lloyd brothers, and their many-faceted interests. The more I learn about Knapp, the more I find a kindred affinity with him. He taught at the Art Academy of Cincinnati where I currently teach, and like myself, he was deeply interested in esoteric subjects.

I am indebted to the marvelous staff at the Lloyd Library and Museum for their support and research assistance. Lead by their wonderful Executive Director, Maggie Heran, the whole staff is warm and helpful. A very special thanks to the assistance of Reference Librarian Alex Herrlein, and Exhibits Curator and Education and Outreach Coordinator Anna Heran, each of who consistently made extraordinary connections between my research topic and the resources available in the library's collection. I've had many great conversations with you all, and I look forward to many more in the future.

Additionally, I would like to thank Ron Decker, author of *A History of the Occult Tarot* (among other books), who has entertained me with endless hours of conversation on these subjects. I also want to thank Yolanda Robinson, Tarot Instructor at the Philosophical Research Society, Edie Shapiro, Archivist at the Philosophical Research Society, Pam Grossman, co-founder of The Observatory and editor for Abraxas Journal, and Justin Moore, host of the radio show "On the Way to the Peak of Normal". Our delightful conversations about alchemy, the Lloyds, Knapp, and related topics bore a significant influence on my project. Thanks also to Kamal Southall, my guide for understanding astral projection as it relates to Sufi mysticism. I'm grateful to you all.

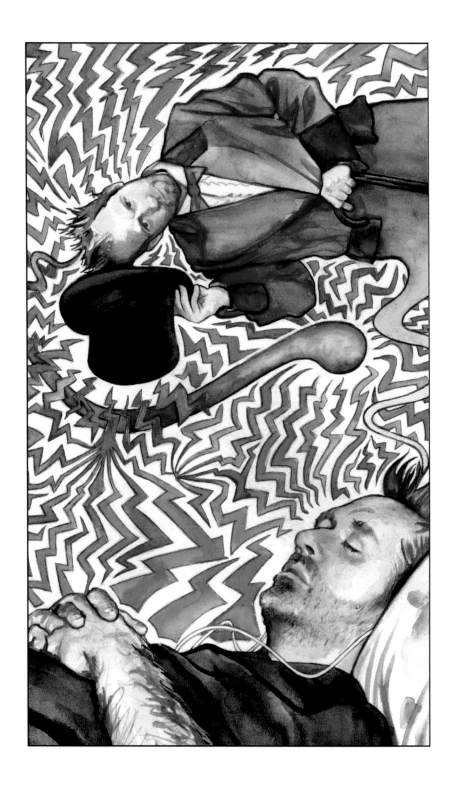

INTRODUCTION

The goal of this book is to establish alchemy as a system for achieving astral projection, the willful projection of the Astral Body into the Astral Plane. I do this by investigating how Renaissance alchemists and magicians discussed astral projection, and by offering fresh ways of interpreting and using the old alchemical symbolism.

There have been a few good (effective) magic books on the subject of astral projection. Most of them rehash Ophiel's brilliant book *The Art and Practice of Astral Projection*. *Alchemy and Astral Projection* takes a different approach. Instead of repeating the same material, I created this book to expand how we use hermetic knowledge to have mystical and magical experiences related to the out of body state.

Though I have had a rich dream life as long as I can remember, my first experiences with astral projection began when I was 17 years old. Like many who have had similar experiences, I consider my out of body experiences to be among the most profound moments of my life. For many of us, it becomes a turning point—a lifelong passion. Now, at the age of 40, I have read countless books in my quest to contextualize these experiences and to develop my ability to further explore the astral realms. These books range from contemporary New Age manuals to ancient Greek philosophy. I am undiscriminating, and will leave no stone unturned. Golden eggs turn up in the most unlikely places.

My quest as a psychonaut is a parallel track to my profession as a visual artist. I've found that the two paths neatly inform one another. It's no secret that creating art can greatly develop the intuitive faculty. I experience more dream recall while painting and drawing than I do during any other activity. At some point, I realized that for my personal fulfillment, these two paths needed to become inextricably fused. That is the spirit of this book. The art herein was not created as an afterthought, but as part of my process for navigating the ideas at hand.

This treatise is divided into three books:

BOOK I, ALCHEMY AND ASTRAL PROJECTION, investigates how Renaissance alchemists and magicians talked about astral projection. Examining passages by Trithemius, Paracelsus, Agrippa, and Heydon, I make a case that alchemy was in large part a system for inducing astral travel. I also look at how their philosophical predecessors from ancient Greece plainly discussed astral projection and related experiences. Of special interest is my treatment of the Microcosm/Macrocosm concept in its relationship to astral projection.

BOOK II, THE SEVEN GATES, explores how the seven stages of alchemical transmutation and their corresponding symbols are used by mystical alchemists to gain access to the Macrocosm (the Astral Plane). I bring new interpretations to the old symbolism, especially regarding the conjunction of the Sun and the Moon.

BOOK III, OCCULT PNEUMATOLOGY, is a short catalogue of entities that exist on the Astral and Elemental Planes according to the writings of Parcelsus and Theosophists such as Charles Leadbeater.

A NOTE ABOUT THE EMBLEMS
Alchemy and magic books differ from most books. In essence, they are part how-to book and part art book, relying heavily on symbols, which become seeds that are sewn in our consciousness. Through time and contemplation, we cultivate these seeds, and they transform us.

The plates in Renaissance alchemy books were intended to conceal knowledge from the uninitiated. This was in part an effort to allay persecution by the establishment. But secrecy was not their only power. Alchemical emblems are a great demonstration of how imagery can provide successive revelation through contemplation. Symbolism is a profound mechanism for transforming consciousness. Illustrations are most effective when they don't simply reiterate the text, but rather respond in conjunction with the text, bringing new meaning to it.

The etymology of *illustrate* is related to the word *illuminate*, or that is, to cast light upon the text. Illumination is suggestive of being profoundly more than a simple explanation. Though my intention with the text is to plainly address the subject with direct, denotative explanation, I also want to leave the reader with images that are more connotative, and thereby capable of unlocking and impressing the content in an indirect, less rational manner. For this reason, I give no rationalistic explanation of my emblems. In many cases, it would be dishonest to do so, because intuition has played a large role in their creation.

Some of the illustrations in this treatise are diagrams of ideas. Other plates are my own artistic contemplations of alchemical concepts. In more than one remarkable instance, I had dreams wherein I worked out compositions for this project. Some of these dreamed compositions became realized as finished paintings that are included in this book. The drawing of the Thoughtform in BOOK III documents an experience I had in the hypnopompic state.

The more informal diagrams drawn in pencil were copied from my personal journals. While I thought about cleaning these up, I reflected on how much enjoyment I receive from the more informally drawn diagrams I have encountered in magic books, and my hope is that you, the reader, will also have an affinity for such renderings. There's something potent about the raw, pictorial diagramming of an idea.

The ink drawing of the man and his psychopomp flying over the rocks was an illustration for *Etidorhpa* by John Augustus Knapp. The painting of water nymphs was also by Knapp. The drawing of the Egyptian ka is from a rare book in the Lloyd Library's collection, *Description de l'Egypte* (1821-1829), documenting Napolean's expeditions to Alexandria. The Starry Salamander and the drawing of Mercury are from *Hermogenes* (1739), by Johann Samuel Heinsii Buchladen, also courtesy of the Lloyd Library.

REGARDING THE RED TEXT
Passages highlighted in red are quotes from Renaissance alchemists and magicians, and ancient Greek philsophers that saliently address the projection of the astral body.

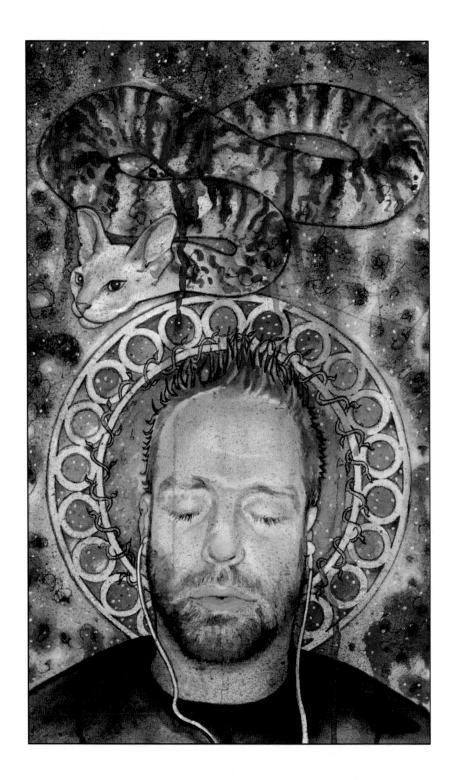

BOOK I

ALCHEMY AND ASTRAL PROJECTION

ECSTATIC TRANCE IN THE HERMETIC TRADITION

ALCHEMY, THE BLACK ART

The alchemy that thrived in Medieval and Renaissance Europe had its roots in the Egyptian and Arab cultures, and also thrived in China. Alchemy, or *al-kimiya* is Arabic, combining *al*, a definitive Arabic article, and *kimiya*, the Greek name for Egypt. *Kimiya* means *black*, and is said to refer to the fertile soil on the banks of the Nile. In this manner, alchemy means the art of Egypt. Another theory is that *black* refers to the art of blacksmithing, which like alchemy is an art of fashioning metals. Chinese alchemy is believed to have grown out of its metallurgical tradition, which in turn grew out of its shamanic tradition.

The Laboratory Alchemist's quest is to discover the powder known as the Philosopher's Stone and use it to make gold. The Philosopher's Stone was not actually a stone, but rather a powder that could transmute base metals into gold or silver. It is believed that this powder speeds the natural maturation of the base metal. Lead, tin, copper, mercury, and silver, are all various stages on an evolutionary course towards becoming gold, the most noble metal. Alchemists were also in search of the elixir of life. *Elixir*, derived from the Arabic *al-iksir*, meaning *dry powder*, a term for medicine that was used for dusting wounds. So we see consonance between the Philosopher's Stone and the Elixir of Life. The terms are often used interchangeably as symbols for the same concepts.

MYSTICAL ALCHEMY

For most, the word *alchemy* conjures images of wayward proto-chemists puffing the flames of their fires in a mad attempt to turn lead into gold and discover the secrets to human immortality. History tells us that, as zany as it sounds, modern chemistry was born of this. The manuscripts we are left with were written with an elaborate symbolism that was clearly intended to cloak the art in secrecy. Further propelling us into even greater depths of fantasy are the elaborate pictorial emblems that illustrate the Renaissance texts, which are populated with unicorns, dragons, and two-headed hermaphrodites. It is undeniable that alchemy was as mystical as it was chemical. Both its verbal and pictorial components are packed with religious and mythological content. The old alchemical tracts tell us repeatedly that the art is an exercise in extracting spirit from matter, purifying the spirit, and then returning it to its matter. Alchemists believed in a spirit that held all things together. It requires us to look at reality not as being comprised of

> "many separate pieces, but as one great and indivisible organism, pervaded by co-existing spiritual powers, whose outward manifestation is the realm of phenomena." (Franz Hartmann, *Paracelsus: Life and Teachings*, 1896)

In fact, there is such an emphasis on the mystical in old alchemy treatises that one can talk about alchemy as being a purely mystical pursuit, with no laboratory component. Over the years, some authors have done just that. My book is in this tradition. It has often been said that there were (and are) two sorts of alchemists: the *laboratory alchemist*, and the *mystical alchemist*, sometimes called the *esoteric alchemist*. This is not to suggest that laboratory alchemy itself lacks a mystical component, but rather addresses the idea that many who read and write alchemy books do not actually engage in laboratory work. Instead, they read the treatises purely for their personal spiritual advancement. Jacob Böehm is a notable example of a mystic who adopted alchemical language to write about his mystical experiences. To be clear, I am not interested in invalidating the notion that alchemists engaged in laboratory pursuits. For many certainly did, and as I write this, there are many lab alchemists alive today who continue to puff the flames.

Today's fashionable opinions regarding alchemical symbolism are guided by psychologist Carl Jung and occult scholar Arthur Edward Waite. Both were mystics, but they also brought the materialist philosophy of their time to the subject. Today's audience interested in alchemy's esoteric symbolism tend to be extraordinary fans of Jung, and of course Waite also has his admirers, though surely not as many. Though both of these men were esotericists, they dismissed or misinterpreted one of the most mystical components of the alchemical symbolism, the symbol of soul flight. Let's begin by looking at their interpretations of the alchemical quest. We'll begin with Waite, for he was the first of the two to begin writing on the topic.

Perhaps most famous for his hand in the *Rider-Waite* tarot deck (possibly the most produced tarot in the English-speaking world), Arthur Edward Waite (1857-1942) wrote on a number of esoteric topics, and translated into English and commented on many important magical and alchemical books, including the works of Paracelsus, Thomas Vaughn, and Eliphas Levi.

Waite's final analysis was that alchemy was neither purely mystical nor purely material, but rather a fusion of the two. He described alchemy as a laboratory process that sought to draw correspondence between the perfection of metals and the perfection of the soul of the alchemist. In other words, as the alchemists attempted to turn lead into gold, they were simultaneously trying to purify their own soul. Seen in this light, the true laboratory alchemist has a mystical bent. The laboratory process doubles as a contemplation of their personal self-development. This prevailing explanation of alchemy was succinctly defined by H. Stanley Redgrove, who relied heavily on Waite. "Alchemy was an attempt to demonstrate experimentally on the material plane the validity of a certain philosophical view of the Cosmos."

He elaborates:

> "Alchemy had its origin in the attempt to apply, in a certain manner, the principles of Mysticism to the things of the physical plane, and was, therefore, of a dual nature, on the one hand spiritual and religious, on the other, physical and material." (*Alchemy Ancient and Modern*, 1910)

Carl Gustav Jung (1875-1961) saw laboratory work as a projection of the alchemist's own process of *Individuation*, his term for becoming an individual self, or that is, becoming whole. To Jung, the alchemist seemed to be putting together the puzzle of his own psychology in material space with the use of his hands. Jung's interest in alchemy was fostered by Herbert Silberer's *Problems of Mysticism and its Symbolism* (1914), later published as *Hidden Symbolism of Alchemy and the Occult Arts*. Like Jung, Silberer was a member of Freud's circle, though he was expelled from the community because of this book. The estrangement is credited with Silberer's suicide. Jung, of course, also diverged from Freud, and went on to write several books on alchemy.

Today, many esotericists see Jung as either reviving or preserving mysticism by clothing it in psychological terminology. However, there is a downside to Jung's psychologizing of alchemical symbolism. He concluded that the ecstatic experience of shamans and alchemists were unconscious phases of their individuation process. Jung interprets the alchemical ascent/descent symbolism as "...an emotional realization of opposites, and this realization gradually leads, or should lead, to their equilibrium." Jung believed that the ascent/descent symbolism in alchemical writings and emblems was an allegorical expression for

> "...the freeing of the soul from the shackles of darkness, or unconsciousness; its ascent to heaven, the widening of consciousness; and finally its return to earth, to hard reality, in the form of the tincture or healing drink, endowed with the powers of the Above." (*Mysterium Coniunctionis*)

This point of view is enticing for the modern individual who wants to use alchemical symbolism as a self-help model for integrating a fragmented psychology. And in fact, there are many books in the self-help genre that take this tack. Unfortunately, in the light of mystical experience, and particularly regarding the astral projection phenomenon, Jung ignored the writings of Renaissance alchemists that explicitly discuss consciously cultivating the ability to leave the body in order to learn information and perform special tasks, such as the following passage by Paracelsus:

> "During sleep the sidereal man may by the power of the imagination be sent out of the physical form, at a distance to act for some purpose."

Many such passages by Paracelsus and other Renaissance alchemists and magicians were available in Jung's time (and we'll be looking at more, momentarily), leaving one to ponder why Jung, who is considered by many to be one of the great modern mystics, would be so materialistically grounded in his interpretation of alchemy's soul-flight symbolism. Perhaps he believed in the reality of soul travel, but was afraid of being shunned by the medical community. Ultimately, towards the end of his life, Jung had a classice NDE (Near Death Experience, a form of OBE).

Prior to Jung and Waite, there were a few writers who had a more mystical interpretation of alchemy's symbolism. Mary Anne Atwood (1817-1910) addressed the relationship between alchemy and soul travel in her remarkable book *A Suggestive Inquiry into Hermetic Mystery* (1850).

Fearing that she had unleashed an ineffable knowledge upon a spiritu-

ally unprepared world, Atwood attempted to gather and burn all of the copies of her book almost immediately following its publication. However, the few copies that escaped the flames were enough to excite interest in the subject, and it has since been republished periodically.

Atwood proposed that alchemy was a method for attaining spiritual ecstasy, or that is, a visionary state in which the alchemist experiences divinity. For Atwood, the alchemist's laboratory was really the human body. Influenced by the mesmerism popular in her time, Atwood speculated that alchemists were mesmerizing one another into having out of body experiences. An adherent of prisca sapientia, Atwood believed that this was a tradition that far predated Renaissance alchemy, tracing the practice to the Eleusinian Mysteries of ancient Greece. It is particularly Atwood's ideas that I am in pursuit of here. Having lived in the shadow of Waite and Jung for a century, she is now all but forgotten.

Another writer who attempted to discuss alchemy as a form of mysticism was Ethan Allen Hitchcock (1798-1870), a Colonel in the U.S. Army who authored scholarly works, including *Remarks on the Sonnets of Shakespeare*, and *Swedenborg a Hermetic Philosopher*. "Transcendental Alchemy" is a concept that can be found in Hitchcock's *Remarks Upon Alchemy and the Alchemists* (1857). This term communicates a belief he shared with Atwood, that alchemy was a mystical process having little if anything to do with physical laboratory work. Hitchcock saw alchemy as a process of moral, behavioral purification. Emblems and formulae are contemplated for the spiritual knowledge they impart, helping alchemists on their quest to purify themselves. Though his theory doesn't specifically address the soul-travel concept, it did influence Silberer, and it set a precedent for Carl Gustav Jung's psychological interpretations of alchemy.

Early in his career, Arthur Edward Waite embraced both Atwood and Hitchcock. He speaks highly of them in his introduction to *Lives of the Alchemystical Philosophers* (1888), but has a dismissive opinion of them by the 1926 publication of his book *The Secret Tradition in Alchemy*.

To support their position that alchemy was first and foremost a laboratory pursuit, Waite, and other writers of alchemy influenced by his thinking, quote the following passage by Paracelsus, who is considered the most influential alchemist and doctor of the Renaissance.

"...they devote themselves diligently to their labour, sweating-whole nights over fiery furnaces. These do not kill the time with empty talk, but find their delight in the laboratory."

Of course this select quote by Paracelsus hardly overturns his extensive magical theories regarding alchemy, magic, the nature of the human soul, and our ability to project it from our body at will. Nonetheless, Waite's interpretation of alchemy informed the current mainstream thought regarding the subject. It's a theory that is neatly aligned with the popular narrative regarding the birth of chemistry, which tells us that we once mixed superstition with laboratory science, but since The Enlightenment, we know better.

HERMETIC MAGIC AND ALCHEMY

Before looking at specific instances where Renaissance Hermeticists and the ancient Greeks discussed astral projection, it is important to review some of the basic mechanisms of the Hermetic worldview as it relates to magic.

Western alchemy is Hermetic, meaning it is based on the Corpus Hermeticum, the pseudepigraphical writings attributed to Hermes Trismegistus (Thrice-greatest Hermes), a prophet related to, but distinct from, the Egyptian god Thoth and the Greek god Hermes. These texts were written in the 2nd and 3rd centuries CE. Hermes Trismegistus is a Mercury-like figure—a conduit between the Microcosm (Earth) and the Macrocosm (heavens). He is a psychopomp, or soul guide, who helps the alchemist move back and forth between the material and spiritual realms.

Hermetic philosophy and magic were influenced by ancient Greek philosophy, particularly Neoplatonism, Gnosticism, and the Greek perception of Egyptian spiritual beliefs. By the Renaissance, alchemy was also influenced by the Jewish Kaballah. Western alchemy was also influenced by Arab cultures.

In the Neoplatonic philosophy, the soul carries our spirit down through the Seven Planetary Spheres to earth. These spheres are not the physical planets, but rather the spiritual planes corresponding to the the seven planets recognized at the time (the five planets visible to the naked eye, plus the Sun and the Moon). Each sphere is a realm that embodies the attributes of the god or goddess lording over it. As our soul descends throught the spheres, we take on the characteristics of each planetary deity, becoming decreasingly divine and increasingly human.

The hierarchical ordering of the seven planets shows variance through the centuries. Trithemius ordered the planets thusly: Saturn, Jupiter, Mars, Sun, Venus, Mercury, Moon.

In the philosophy, there are four tangible elements, Earth, Water, Air, and Fire. The fifth alchemical element is Quintescence or spirit, also referred to as Azoth, or Philosphical Mercury. This is the Macrocosmic aether that comprises the heavens above the terrestrial sphere. There is also a little Quintessence in everything on the material plane.

This is how sympathetic magic works. The spirit in things on the material or Microcosmic plane corresponds with the spirit that comprises the heavens, or Macrocosmic plane. As above, so below. Like attracts like. Everything on earth corresponds to one of the seven planets. Each planet is governed by an angel. Material things are marked with signatures that are clues that inform us about a thing's corresponding planetary influences. Alchemists believed that through prayer and the use of the Imaginative Faculty, we are able to identify and unlock the meanings of these signatures and employ the appropriate angel to wield its influence to our benefit. As Paracelsus explained:

> "The soul does not perceive the external or internal physical construction of herbs and roots, but it intuitively perceives their powers and virtues, and recognizes at once their signature."

This magical philosophy is not to be separated from medicine. Paracelsus wrote clearly about how the two entertwine.

> "I have reflected a great deal upon the magical powers of the soul of man, and I have discovered a great many secrets in Nature, and I will tell you that he only can be a true physician who has acquired this power."

Paracelsus emphasized doing over believing. In the following passage, he eloquently discerns between spiritual faith and spiritual knowledge, and reveals the crux of his magical philosophy:

> "The exercise of true magic does not require any ceremonies or conjurations, or the making of circles or signs; it requires neither benedictions nor maledictions in words, neither verbal blessings nor curses; it only requires a strong faith in the omnipotent power of all good, that can accomplish everything if it acts through a human mind being in harmony with it, and without which nothing useful can be accomplished. True magic power consists in true faith, but true faith rests in spiritual knowledge, and without that kind of knowledge there can be no faith. If I know that divine wisdom can accomplish a certain thing through me, I have the true holy faith but if I merely fancy or suppose that a thing might be possible, or if I attempt to persuade myself that I believe in its possibility, such a belief is no knowledge, and confers no faith. No one can have a true faith in a thing which is not true, because such a 'faith' would be merely a belief or opinion based upon ignorance of truth."

According to ancient Greek philosophers and Renaissance alchemists and magicians, true spiritual knowledge is gained through direct experience with the divine--soul travel to the Macrocosm. The only way to know that a greater spiritual reality exists is to experience it.

The use of the soul, or astral body, is integral to all Hermetic magic. It is used to mediate energy between the Microcosm and the Macrocosm. Four magico-mystical functions of the astral body are described by Renaissance alchemists and magicians:

1. It intuitively absorbs information from the Macrocosm.

2. It leaves the physical body to acquire information from the celestial influences (angels) and the spirits of other magicians. Paracelsus believed that this happens automatically and unintentionally during sleep, and also that the astral body can be projected by force of will.

3. It is consciously sent out to convey information to another person.

4. It is consciously sent out for the purpose of mystical union with its divine, Macrocosmic source (enosis).

MYSTICAL TRANCE IN ANCIENT GREECE

The term *ecstasy*, derived from the Ancient Greek ἔκστασις, *to be or stand outside oneself,* has often been used to discuss astral projection. The ancient Greeks used the label *thiasos* for worshippers of various cults who engaged in ecstasy.

The Neoplatonic philosopher Thomas Taylor, in his thesis *Eleusinian and Bacchic Mysteries* (c. 1790), compiled a few examples of ecstasy found in the writings of the ancient Greek philosophers. Plato (c. 428 - 348 BCE) wrote of the climax of his initiation into the Mysteries.

> "But it was then lawful to survey the most splendid beauty, when we obtained, together with that blessed choir, this happy vision and contemplation. And we indeed enjoyed this blessed spectacle together with Jupiter; but others in conjunction with some other god; at the same time being initiated in those Mysteries, which it is lawful to call the most blessed of all Mysteries. And these divine Orgies were celebrated by us, while we possessed the proper integrity of our nature, we were freed from the molestations of evil which otherwise await us in a future period of time. Likewise, in consequence of this divine initation, we became spectators of entire, simple, immovable, and blessed visions, resident in pure light and were ourselves pure and immaculate, being liberated from this surrounding vestment, which we denominate body, and to which we are now bound like an oyster to its shell."

Proclus (412 – 485 AD) elaborated upon Plato's description of initiation.

> "That the initiation and epopteia (the vailing and the revealing) are symbols of ineffable silence, and of union with mystical natures through intelligible visions."

This lead Taylor to conclude that the *Revealing,* or culminating experience of the Eleusinian rites was a symbolic substitute of a true visionary experience. The true experience was an ecstatic vision that occurs in an out of body state.

> "Now, from all this, it may be inferred, that the most sublime

"WE LEAPED OVER GREAT INEQUALITIES."

part of the epopteia or final revealing, consisted in beholding the gods themselves invested with a resplendent light; and that this was symbolical of those transporting visions, which the virtuous soul will constantly enjoy in a future state; and of which it is able to gain some ravishing glimpses, even while connected with the cumbrous vestment of body."

The most influential Neoplatonic philosopher was Plotinus (c. 204-270), who elaborated upon Plato's writings to establish a more mystical Platonic philosophy. Plotinus wrote that the Infinite can be experienced through the soul of man, and that this experience was one of ecstasy in which a person literally steps outside himself. He said that he did this many times. In a letter to Flaccus, Plotinus wrote:

> "You ask, how can we know the Infinite? I answer, not by reason. It is the office of reason to distinguish and define. The Infinite, therefore, cannot be ranked among its objects. You can only apprehend the Infinite by a faculty superior to reason, by entering into a state in which you are your finite self no longer—in which the divine essence is communicated to you. This is ecstasy. It is the liberation of your mind from its finite consciousness. Like only can apprehend like; when you thus cease to be finite, you become one with the Infinite. In the reduction of your soul to its simplest self, its divine essence, you realize this union—this identity. But this sublime condition is not of permanent duration. It is only now and then that we can enjoy this elevation (mercifully made possible for us) above the limits of the body and the world. I myself have realized it but three times as yet, and Porphyry hitherto not once. All that tends to purify and elevate the mind will assist you in this attainment, and facilitate the approach and the recurrence of these happy intervals. There are, then, different roads by which this end may be reached."

Porphyry would later write that he was present no less than four times when Plotinus experienced enosis, and that he himself experienced it, though only once at sixty-eight years of age.

The "faculty superior to reason" Plotinus refers us to is Wisdom. Wisdom is divine knowledge, as distinct from worldly knowledge. Obtaining it is integral to the process of spiritual purification. It is obtained directly from the divine through the Wisdom Faculty. The quote by John Uri Lloyd at the top of my Acknowledgments page states that accessing the Wisdom Faculty was the final possibility of alchemy, and that it will help us travel to planes beyond material reality. Lloyd pulled the term "Wisdom-faculty" from his personal copy of A. E. Waite's *Lives of Alchemystical Philosophers*. Waite's mention and discussion of the term is brief.

> "In addition to the faculties which he commonly exerts to communicate with the material universe, man possesses within him the germ of a higher faculty, the revelation and evolution of which give intuitive knowledge of the hidden springs of nature. This Wisdom-faculty operates in a magical manner, and constitutes an alliance with the Omniscient Nature, so that the illuminated understanding of its possessor perceives the structure of the universe, and enjoys free perspicacity of thought in universal consciousness."

Waite, like many others, interpreted this faculty to be a sort of divine intuition. Momentarily, we will see that Renaissance alchemists preferred to say that the willful projection of the astral body occurs through the exercise of another faculty referred to as *Imagination*.

There are other notable examples of astral projection in ancient Greece, such as the case of Arisdeu, which was documented by Plutarch (c. 46-120 AD). Arisdeu was a disreputable member of his community until he suffered coma-inducing head trauma. He was believed to be dead, and came to just prior to his burial. During his coma, he had an OBE (or perhaps more accurately, an NDE), in which he met a spirit guide who toured him around the spirit world. Plutarch wrote that Arisdeu's experience changed his moral character for the better.

ZOSIMOS OF PANOPOLIS

Hermetic alchemy does not occur long after ancient Greece. Notable is Zosimos of Panopolis, a Gnostic alchemist of the late 3rd-early 4th centuries. Zosimos' writings are extremely mystical in nature. He claimed that metallurgy was taught to men by the fallen angels, and documented his visions, which he interpreted to be spiritual guidance regarding the various stages of the alchemical transmutation process.

ASTRAL PROJECTION IN THE RENAISSANCE

While Plotinus' and Porphyry's out of body experiences in ancient Greece far precede the height of alchemy in Renaissance Europe, the theme is taken up in Renaissance books, some of which refer directly back to antiquity. Plotinus' work, Plato's work, and the *Corpus Hermeticum* were all translated by Marsilio Ficino (1433-1499), a man who Paracelsus considered Italy's finest doctor. Hired by Cosimo de' Medici, Ficino was the leader of the Neoplatonic Academy and a key figure of the Renaissance. Ficino himself a magus, wrote his own book of celestial magic, *De Vita Coelitus Comparanda* (How to Fit Your Life to the Heavens).

Though not Christian, Plotinus wrote about God as a trinity (One, Soul, and Spirit). His concept of the tri-part man found fertile soil in Renaissance humanistic consciousness, which blended Greek philosophy with Christian theology, and directed the manner in which they discussed astral projection. Specifically, alchemists found consonance between Plotinus' tri-part human and the three primaries of alchemy: salt, sulfur, and mercury, which are commonly interpreted as representing the body, soul, and spirit, respectively. Atwood noted this in her *Suggestive Inquiry*, and it informed her theory that alchemy was an unbroken esoteric tradition that bridged the two periods.

Atwood highlighted one particularly revealing tract by Michael Sendivogius, *New Light of Alchemy* (1608):

> "That nature, having her proper light, is by the shadowy body of sense, hidden rom our eyes; but if, says he, the light of nature doth enlighten any one, presently the cloud is taken away from before his eyes, and without any let, he can behold the point of our loadstone, answering to each centre of the beams, viz. of the sun and moon philosophical,) for so far doth the light of nature penetrate and discover inward things; the body of man is a shadow of the seed of nature, and as man's body is covered with a garment, so is man's nature covered with a body."

New Light of Alchemy states that alchemists aren't covetous of gold or silver, but for knowledge of not only nature, but the divine, and that they are:

"...willing to speak of these things sparingly, only, and figuratively, lest those divine mysteries, by which nature is illustrated, should be discovered to be unworthy; which thou, if thou knowest how to know thyself, and art not of a stiff neck, mayest easily comprehend, who art created after the likeness of the great world, yea after the image of God. Thou has in thy body the anatomy of the whole world, and all thy members answer to some celestials; let, therefore, the searcher of this Sacred Science know that the soul in man, the lesser world or microcosm, substituting the place of its centre, is the king, and is placed in the vital spirit in the purest blood. That governs the mind, and the mind the body, governing all its motions, hath a far greater operation out of the body, because out of the body it absolutely reigns; and in this respect, it differs from the life of other creatures which have only spirit and not the soul of Deity."

The previous quote is particularly revealing about the role astral projection plays in alchemy.

TRITHEMIUS
(1462-1516)

To understand the proliferation of the mystical elements of alchemy in the Renaissance, and of the spread of magic, it's important to know that Paracelsus, the most influential alchemist of his time, and Cornelius Agrippa, the most influential magus of his time, were both students of the famed abbot and notorious magus Trithemeus of Sponheim. Trithemeus wrote a number of books, the most famous of them being the *Steganographia (published posthumously in 1606)*, now commonly understood to be a handbook of cryptography in the guise of a book on astral magic, or that is, the art of angel and demon conjuration. Whether or not the book was meant to operate as both a book of cryptography and a magic book is subject to debate. Regardless, there is no doubt that Trithemius was a very mystical man with a bent for magic. In a footnote in his book *Paracelsus and the Substance of his Teachings*, Franz Hartmann wrote

"Johannes Tritheim, Abbot of Spanheim, one of the greatest alchemists, theologians, and astrologers, a learned and highly esteemed man, makes some remarks in his book (printed at Passau, 1506) that may help to throw some light on the perplexing subject of alchemy. He says: "The art of divine magic consists of the ability to perceive the essence of things in the light of Nature, and by using the soul-powers of the spirit to produce material things from the unseen universe (Akasa), and in such must be brought together and made to act harmoniously. The spirit of Nature is a unity, creating and forming everything, and by acting through the instrumentality of man it may produce wonderful things. Such processes take place according to law. You will learn the law by which these things are accomplished, if you learn to know yourself. You will know it by the power of the spirit that is in yourself, and accomplish it by mixing your spirit with the essence that comes out of yourself. If you wish to succeed in such a work, you must know how to separate spirit and life in Nature, and moreover, to separate the astral soul in yourself and to make it tangible, and then the substance of the soul will appear visibly and tangibly, rendered objective by the power of the spirit. Christ speaks of the salt, and the salt is of a threefold nature. Gold is of a threefold nature, and there is an ethereal, a fluid, and a material gold It is the same gold, only in three different states; and gold in one state may be made into gold in another state. But such mysteries should not be divulged, because the fool and scoffer will laugh at it, and to him who is covetous they will be a temptation."

PARACELSUS
(1493-1541)

In his time, Philippus von Hohenheim, known as Paracelsus, was the most renowned and controversial physician alive. His medicine was alchemy, and he was believed by many to work miracles. He also had his detractors, and vicious rumors and speculations about his character kept him moving about.

I have already quoted a few of Paracelsus' thoughts on intuition, medicine, and magic. Such passages are very much the sort of intuitive mysticism that A. E. Waite highlighted when he wrote about alchemy. But a discussion on intuition does not summarize Paracelsus' spiritual worldview. In his writings, he addresses spirit travel several times, and sundry entities we might encounter on the astral plane.

"There are some persons whose nature is so spiritual, and their souls so exalted, that they can approach the highest spiritual sphere at a time when their bodies are asleep."

Paracelsus also wrote that during astral projection we are able to transmit information to another person. It's interesting to see how he distinguishes between the imaginative faculty and *fancy*. Clearly our contemporary use of the word *imagination* is watered down. It is through the exercise of our Imaginative Faculty that we are able to control the astral projection experience.

"The spirit is the master, imagination the tool, and thee body the plastic material. Imagination is the power by which the will forms sidereal entities out of thoughts. Imagination is not fancy, which latter is the cornerstone of superstitious foolishness. The imagination of man becomes pregnant through desire, and gives birth to deeds. Every one may regulate and educate his imagination so as to come thereby into contact with spirits, and be taught by them. Spirits desiring to act upon man act upon his imagination, and they therefore make often use of his dreams for the purpose of acting upon him. During sleep the sidereal man may by the power of the imagination be sent out of the physical form, at a distance to act for some purpose. No place is too far for the imagination to go, and the imagination of one man can impress that of another, wherever it reaches" (Philosophia Sagax).

Abbe Louis Constant (1810-1875), a Frenchman better known by his magical name, Eliphas Levi, explained that we have a luminous body within us that is the mirror of our imagination--a plastic medium that reproduces forms corresponding to ideas. This medium is nourished by the Astral Light. The magician draws the Astral Light down from the heavens and charges himself and his objects with this substance in order to perform his magic. The alchemists' Azoth is equivalent to Eliphas Levi's Astral Light. This luminous body is the human soul, as distinguishable from the human spirit.

Again, we are speaking of the *Imaginative Faculty*. For most people in our society today, the imaginal is cast to the realm of the frivolous. It is that which is not real (material), and therefore, it does not matter, with perhaps the exception of its contribution to our technological advancement or our entertainment. While we have some vague cultural value assigned to the idea of creativity, few value, or partake in, the exercise of the imaginative faculty. Most rare is the form of a regimented program for imagination development such as that exercised by a magical order of the Hermetic tradition, like The Golden Dawn of the late nineteenth century.

In the ancient wisdom traditions, a cultivated Imaginative Faculty can render prophecy. Moses Maimonides, a Spanish Sephardic Jewish rabbi of the 12th century wrote:

> "PROPHECY is, in truth and reality, an emanation sent forth by the Divine Being through the medium of the Active Intellect, in the first instance to man's rational faculty, and then to his imaginative faculty; it is the highest degree and greatest perfection man can attain: it consists in the most Perfect development of the imaginative faculty. Prophecy is a faculty that cannot in any way be found in a person, or acquired by man, through a culture of his mental and moral faculties: for even if these latter were as good and perfect as possible, they would be of no avail, unless they were combined with the highest natural excellence of the imaginative faculty."
> (*Guide for the Perplexed*, 12th C.)

THE MACROCOSM IS THE ASTRAL PLANE

There is a general misunderstanding that the Hermetic Macrocosm is some abstract notion of the greater cosmic universe. Paracelsus' discussion of the Macrocosm reveals that it is equivalent to what Theosophists call the Astral Plane. He discussed the Macrocosm as a place that can be visited, a shadow land that is one part material and one part spiritual. Our Astral Body is a Microcosm, a small world made of the same material that composes the Astral Plane, which, Paracelsus tells us, is what allows us to enter the Macrocosm and interact with it.

> "Neither the external nor the astral man is the real man, but the real man is the spiritual soul in connection with the Divine Spirit. The astral soul is the shadow of the body, illumined by the spirit, and it therefore resembles man. It is neither material

nor immaterial, but partakes of the nature of each. The inner man is formed out of the same Limbus as the Macrocosm, and he is therefore able to participate in all the wisdom and knowledge of all creatures, angels, and spirits, and learn to understand their attributes. He may learn from the Macrocosm the meaning of the symbols by which he is surrounded, in the same manner as he acquires the language of his parents; because his own soul is the quintessence of everything in creation, and is connected sympathetically with the whole of Nature; and therefore every change that takes place in the Macrocosm can be sensed by the ethereal essence surrounding his spirit, and it may come to the consciousness and comprehension of man."

AGRIPPA
(1486-1535)

Heinrich Cornelius Agrippa's *Three Books of Occult Philosophy* (1533, dedicated to Trithemeus) were a consolidation of the Neoplatonic magic available at the time. The only information lacking was the actual processes of ceremonial magic, which were published after Agrippa's death in the form of Book IV (though its authorship has been subject to argument). Agrippa continues to be influential on magical theory.

Many topics are discussed in the collection of the three books. My source, the translation into English by John French (1651), is 583 pages long. In it we find discussions on geomancy, goetia (demon evocation), "the Cablalie of the Jews" (Kaballah), and many other subjects. Throughout the books, there are many explanations of the relationship of the soul and spirit to the body, the nature of our attending genius and demon, and so forth. Agrippa's approach to these subjects, like Paracelsus', is very complicated. Many have described Neoplatonic magic and alchemy as convoluted and self-contradicting philosophies. I think it would be more accurate to state that the philosophy is Mercurial and organic.

Many explanations of soul travel are peppered throughout Book III of Agrippa's *Three Books of Occult Philosophy*. Agrippa put forth an elaborate theory regarding how a purified soul intuitively absorbs divine wisdom.

"So souls going out of the body, so Angels, so Demons speak:

and what man doth with a sensible voyce [voice], they do by impressing the conception of the speech in those to whom they speak, after a better manner then if they should express it by an audible voyce. So the Platonists say that Socrates perceived his Demon by sense indeed, but not of this body, but by the sense of the etherial body concealed in this: after which manner Avicen believes the Angels were wont to be seen, and heard by the Prophets: That instrument, whatsoever the vertue be, by which one spirit makes known to another spirit what things are in his minde, is called by the Apostle Paul the tongue of Angels. Yet oftentimes also they send forth an audible voyce, as they that cryed at the ascension of the Lord, Ye men of Galile [Galilee], why stand ye there gazing into the heaven? And in the old law they spake with divers of the Fathers with a sensible voyce, but this never but when they assumed bodies. But with what senses those spirits and Demons hear our invocations, and prayers, and see our ceremonies, we are altogether ignorant. For there is a spirituall body of Demons everywhere sensible by nature, so that it toucheth, seeth, heareth, without any medium, and nothing can be an impediment to it: Yet neither do they perceive after that manner as we do with different organs, but haply as sponges drink in water, so do they all sensible things with their body, or some other way unknown to us; neither are all animals endowed with those organs; for we know that many want ears, yet we know they perceive a sound, but after what manner we know not."

Another passage:

"Plato defines this by alienation, and binding; for he abstracts from those by which the corporeal senses are stirred up, and being estranged from an animal man, adheres to a deity from whom it receives those things which it cannot search into by its own power; for when the minde is free, and at liberty, the reines of the body being loosed, and going forth as out of a close prison, transcends the bonds of the members, and nothing hindering of it, being stirred up by its own instigations, and instigated by a divine spirit, comprehends all things, and foretells future things.

Much more transparent conversation about astral projection can be found in Chapter L of Agrippa's Book III, titled "Of rapture, and extasie, and soothsayings, which happen to them which are taken with the falling sickness, or with a swoune, or to them in an agonie. " As this chapter is completely about ecstasy, I reprint it in full below, pausing occasionally to point out the relationship between the text and the topic at hand.

> "A rapture is an abstraction, and alienation, and an illustration of the soul proceeding from God, by which God doth again retract the soul, being falled from above to hell, from hell to heaven. The cause of this is in us a continual contemplation of sublime things, which as far as it conjoyns with a most profound intention of the mind, the soul to incorporeal wisdom, doth so far recall it self with its vehement agitations from things sensible and the body, and (as Plato saith) in such a manner sometimes, that it even flieth out of the body, and seemeth as it were dissolved:…"

Note the description of the astral body as "dissolved". In BOOK II of my treatise, I compare similar passages to the alchemical transmutation phases Solutio and Sublimatio. Agrippa's chapter continues with clarification that the divine knowledge is not just absorbed intuitively, but also during astral projection:

> "…even as Aurelius Austin reporteth concerning a Priest of Calamia; (or whom we have made mention before) he lay (saith he) most like unto a dead man, without breath; and when he was burnt with fire and wounded, he felt it not; so great therefore is the command of the soul: viz. when it hath obtained its own nature, and is not oppressed by the allurements of the senses, that by its own power it suddenly ascendeth, not only remaining in the body, but even sometimes loosed from its fetters, and flyeth forth of the body to the supercelestiall habitations, where now it being most nigh, and most like to God, and made the receptacle of divine things, it is filled with the divine Light and Oracles."

In this following passage, we don't just receive a roll call of ancient writers who experienced ecstasy, but also a key passage that tells us Agrippa interpreted Hermes Trismegistus, the legendary author of *The Emerald Tablet*, the foundational text upon which all Western alchemy is based, as telling us that we must have an out of body experience.

> "Whence Zoroastes saith, thou must ascend to the light it self, and to the beams of the Father, whence thy soul was sent thee, clothed with very much mind; and Trismegisius saith, it is necessary that thou ascend above the heavens, and be far from the quire of spirits; and Pythagoras saith, if thou by leaving the body shalt pass into the spacious heavens, thou shalt be an immortall god. So we read that Hermes, Socrates, Xenocrates, Plato, Plotine, Heraclitus, Pythagoras and Zoroastes, were wont to abstract themselves by rapture, and so to learn the knowledge of many things: also we read in Herodotus, that there was in Proconnesus a Philosopher of wonderful knowledge, called Atheus, whose soul sometimes went out of the body, and after the visitation of places far remote, returned again into the body more learned: Pliny reporteth the same thing, that the soul of Harman Clazomenius was wont to wander abroad, his body being left, and to bring true tidings of things very far off"

As Donald Tyson noted in a footnote in his translation of the *Three Books of Occult Philosophy*, the following passage most likely refers to the legendary Siberian shamans.

> "...and there are even to this day in Norway and Lapland very many who can abstract themselves three whole dayes from their body, and being returned declare many things which are afar off; and in the meantime it is necessary to keep them, that not any living creature come upon them or touch them; otherwise they report that they cannot return into their body."

Here Agrippa states that to leave the body is to become omniscient:

> "Therefore we must know, that (according to the doctrine of the Aegyptians,) seeing the soul is a certain spirituall light, when it is loosed from the body, it comprehendeth every place and time, in such a manner as a light inclosed in a Lanthern, which being open, diffuseth it self every where, and faileth not any where, for it is every where, and continually; and Cicero in his book of Divination saith, neither doth the soul of man at any time divine, when it is so loosed that it hath indeed little or

nothing to do with the body; when therefore it shall attain to that state, which is the supream degree of contemplative perfection, then it is rapt from all created species, and understandeth not by acquired species, but by the inspection of the Ideas, and it knoweth all things by the light of the Ideas:"

The next bit of text touches on OBEs that are also Near Death Experiences.

"...of which light Plato saith few men are partakers in this life; but in the hands of the gods, all: also they who are troubled with the syncope and falling sickness, do in some manner imitate a rapture, and in these sicknesses sometimes as in a rapture do bring forth prophesie, in which kind of prophesying we read that Hercules and many Arabians were very excellent, and there are certain kinds of soothsayings, which are a middle betwixt the confines of naturall predictions, and supernaturall Oracles, viz. which declare things to come from some excess of passion, as too much love, sorrow, or amongst frequent sights, or in the agony of death, as in Statius, of the mother of Achilles;--------Nor she without parents dear Under the glassie gulf the oars did fear.

For there is in our minds a certain perspicuous power, and capable of all things, but encumbred and hindred by the darkness of the body and mortality, but after death it having acquired immortality, and being freed from the body it hath full and perfect knowledge. Hence it cometh to pass, that they who are nigh to death, and weakened by old age, have sometimes somewhat of an unaccustomed light, because the soul being less hindred by the senses, understandeth very acutely, and being now as it were a little relaxed from its bands, is not altogether subject to the body, and being as it were nigher to the place, to the which it is about to go, it easily perceiveth revelations, which being mixed with its agonies, are then offered to it; whence Ambrose in his book of the belief of the resurrection, saith, Which being free in the aerial motion, knoweth not whither it goeth, and whence it cometh; yet we know that it superviveth the body, and that it being freed, the chains of its senses being cast off, freely discerneth those things which it saw not before, being in the body,

> which we may estimate by the example of those who sleep, whose mind being quiet, their bodies being as it were buried, do elevate themselves to higher things, and do declare to the body the visions of things absent, yea even of celestial things."

That concludes Chapter L of Agrippa's *BOOK III*. But there are more quotes from Agrippa that are worth reproducing here. We have letters that Agrippa wrote that summarize the key to magic. One particular letter, addressed to Aurelius de Aquapendente, reveals that Agrippa believed that in order for us to know the occult secrets during life, we must die. This was Agrippa's manner of writing about ecstasy. During the out of body experience, it is as though the body is dead, while the mind is alive.

> "For how shall he that hath lost himself in mortal dust, and ashes, find God? How shall he apprehend spiritual things that is swallowed up in flesh and blood? Can man see God, and live? What fruit shall a grain of corn bear if it be not first dead? For we must dye, I say dye to the world, and to the flesh, and all senses, and to the whole man animal, who would enter into these closets of secrets, not because the body is separated from the soul, but because the soul leaves the body: of which death Paul wrote to the Collossians: Ye are dead, and your life is hid with Christ: And elsswhere he speaks more clearly of himself. I know a man, whether in the body, or out of the body I cannot tell, God knows, caught up unto the third heaven, &c. I say by this death, pretious in the sight of God, we must dye, which happens to few, and perhaps not alwaies. For very few whom God loves, and are vertuous, are made so happy. And first those that are born, not of flesh and blood, but of God. Secondly those that are dignified to it by the blessing of nature, and the heavens at their birth. The rest endeavour by merits, and art, of which more fully when I see you. "

HEYDON
(1629-c. 1667)

John Heydon's *Theomagia* (1633) is a book of celestial magic that details the planetary spirits that provide knowledge to the magician. He makes it clear numerous times that knowledge is imparted while in the astral.

"This course therefore she now taketh: seeing she may not her self step forth and range abroad to see things; she craves leave and takes the help of the Soul, which after the visitation of places far remote, returns again into the Body more Learned, by the help of his Servants, which receives the tidings of things brought very far off."

"After that a man hath abstracted himself from his Body, how to do it, I shall tell you in its due place…"

"For saith he, in Sleep the Spirits of the Brains be still and quiet, but the Soul wanders with me, whilst the parts of the Body all cease at once, and nothing but Air is left to exercise the Organs…"

"…Whence it is possible, naturally, and far from all manner of superstition, no other spirit coming between, that a man shall be able in a very short time, to signifie his mind unto another man, abiding at a very great and unknown distance from him; although he can not precisely give an estimate of the time when it is yet of necessity it must be within twenty four hours, and I myself know how to do it, and have taught many, and they have often done it; also when certaine appearances, not only spiritual, but also natural do flow forth from things, viz. by a certain kind of flowings forth of bodies from bodies, and do gather strength in the Aire, they offer, and shew themselves to us, as well through light as Motion, as well to the sight as to other senses, and sometimes work wonderful things upon us, by the help of Figures, Ideas, and their Rulers;"

In the previous quote, Heydon indicates that certain "Rulers" (angels) may be summoned to assist us during the out of body state. He also states that he is forbidden to reveal too much of the process. "But our Genius forbids as to teach these secret truths to those that may divulge them publickly…" Nonetheless, the keen eye will note that he identifies Camael as an angel of particular help. I elaborate on this in BOOK II, in the section GATE THREE: SEPARATIO.

CHINESE AND INDIAN ALCHEMY

Because this book is focused on the Hermetic tradition, I have, to this point, focused on documents from the Western world. It is important to mention that there are clear connections to be made between Hermetic alchemy and both Chinese Taoist Alchemy and Indian Alchemy. Western alchemy has commonly been called "The yoga of the West" because of these similarities.

All three strains of alchemy have ancient origins. All seek the key to immortality through the creation of elixirs. Many alchemical symbols are shared between the East and the West, as will be seen in portions of BOOK II of this treatise. Chinese Taoist alchemy has an internal work (Neidan) and an external work (Waidan). Neidan is about working with the energies already present in the body through meditation. By the late 17th century, Taoist alchemy had become a purely mystical pursuit.

Many illustrations of astral projection can be found in Chinese scrolls. For example, mid-17th century scrolls show the "Immortal" Li Tieguai releasing his soul from his body for a journey.

Below is a notable quote from the book *Tan Ching Yao Chueh*, attributed to Sun Ssu-mo (AD 581–after 673), that specifically addresses spirit travel:

> "I have read in succession the lore books of ancient times; they agree that, without exception, cases of men's bodies sprouting feathered wings and rising weightlessly in flight were due to the taking of elixirs. Never did I read or speak of these things without feeling an ardent longing in my heart. My sole regret was that the divine Way is so remote, the pathway through the clouds so inaccessible. I gazed in vain at azure heaven, not knowing how to ascend it. I began to practice the techniques of preparing elixirs by cyclical transformation and of fixing substances in the fire, and the formulas for making potable jade and liquid gold."

Nathan Sivin, in *Chinese Alchemy: Preliminary Studies* (1968), compiled an extensive list of Sun Ssu-mo's elixirs. Notably: Grand Unity Spirit-Summoning Elixir, Spirit-Returning Elixir, Resurrection Elixir, Envoy Elixir for Communion with Spirits, Elixir of Ascent into the Roseate Clouds, Crimson-Colored Empyrean-Roaming Elixir, Beaming Moonlight Elixir, Great Cyclically Transformed Elixir, Supernatural Flight

Elixir of Grandee Chang, Elixir of Ascension as an Immortal, Elixir of Ma the Immortal's Ascension to Heaven in the Broad Daylight, etc. These elixirs were probably not hallucinogenic in nature, but rather intended to calm the mind and balance the alchemist's physical and spiritual energies to prepare them for astral travel. The key to ecstasy rests in our ability to relax our body to sleep while our mind stays awake.

MESMERISM

Mary Anne Atwood believed that the alchemists and their ancient Greek predecessors were mesmerizing one another. Mesmerism, a process similar to hypnotism, though distinguishable from it, was named for the German physician Franz Anton Mesmer (1734-1815). One aspect of Mesmerism that distinguishes it from hypnotism is the concept of *Animal Magnetism*, an invisible life force, which could be likened to qi (chi) of Chinese culture, prana in the Hindu religion, the Azoth of the alchemists, and Levi's Astral Light. History does seem to indicate that Mesmerism as a process existed prior to Mesmer's time, and was perhaps known by other terms.

Grillot de Givry wrote in his book *Witchcraft, Magic & Alchemy* (1929) that the 17th century referred to Mesmerism as *somnific witchcraft*. Givry reproduced an image from Pere Guaccius' book *Compendium Maleficarum* (Milan, 1626), and describes it: "It shows three gossips, one of whom is a witch, occupied in making passes over a woman asleep on a bed." The image is from a chapter titled De Meleficio Somnifico. Givry also mentioned that Agrippa addresses the subject in Book I, chapter 1, quoting the following passage:

> "Fascination is a binding or charm which passes from the mind of the sorcerer through the eyes and to the heart of the one he is bewitching, and sorcery is an instrument of the mind—namely, a pure, shining, subtle vapour proceeding from the purest blood engendered by the heat of the heart, which does continually send rays of a like nature through the eyes. You must know, therefore, that men grow bewitched when they look continuously straight into the eyes of another and that the eyes of the two then fasten themselves strongly to one another, and light of eye also to light of eye; mind then joining to mind and carrying flashes to it and fixing them upon it."

Though it is not necessary for people to work with partners to achieve the trance state, many have found it useful, as attested by the interest Mesmer generated.

ASTRAL PROJECTION IN THE MODERN MAGICAL REVIVAL

The afforementioned Golden Dawn studied both alchemy and astral projection, among other occult topics. Waite was a member of this magical order, as were many other notable figures of his day, including William Butler Yeats, Maud Gonne, Evelyn Underhill, and Arthur Machen. Though the order sought to find correspondences between alchemy, astrology, the qabalah, and other bodies of knowledge, no surviving documents show that they discussed a significant relationship between alchemy and astral projection. I mention this because, as we move on to the second part of this treatise, I will be making connections between alchemical symbolism and various aspects of the visionary experience.

It's curious to note the documents for study known as the Flying Rolls that circulated among members of the second order of The Golden Dawn. One of these, Flying Roll VII, was based on Wynn Westcott's lecture on alchemy, delivered in 1890. Several Flying Rolls (Rolls IV, XI, XXV, XXX, XXVI, XXXIII) were devoted to astral projection. These writings were compiled by Francis King in his book *Astral Projection, Ritual Magic, and Alchemy* (1971). Although that title might suggest crossover between these subjects, there is no such analysis found in the book, and rightly so, for the intention of the book was to compile and present these documents to a larger public.

"Astra", in the writings of Paracelsus, is Latin for "stars". When he wrote of the "astra", he wasn't referring to the physical bodies of the planets, but rather to the spiritual planes which are represented by the stars. These planes have also been called "mental states". Experiencing these alternate states of awareness has been referred to by various terms over the years. The Golden Dawn had a process it called *Rising on the Planes*, a structure to the vision quest that involved traveling up and through these planes.

Astral Projection became a point of controversy for the Golden Dawn, and has been credited with some of the schisms within the organization, leading to the original order's demise.

BOOK II

THE SEVEN GATES

SOUL FLIGHT AND ALCHEMICAL SYMBOLISM

THE SEVEN GATES

Mystical alchemy uses the alchemical stages of the transmutation process as keys, or gates, through which the alchemist gains access to the Macrocosm (the Astral Plane).

The number and ordering of these stages vary among alchemy tracts. The most common number of transmutation phases in Western alchemy is seven, which corresponds to the seven metals.

The number seven has an important place in Western mysticism. Jacob Boehme, a Christian mystic who worked with the language of alchemical symbolism, believed that each person has seven spirits that correspond to seven planes of existence. The Theosophists also believed in The Septenary in Man. St. Teresa of Avila, known for her mastery of religious ecstasy, divided her experiences into seven mansions. Many such examples could be cited.

In my following exploration of alchemical symbolism as it relates to astral projection, I have chosen a common set and ordering of transmutation phases. They are, in descending order:

7. Coagulatio—Sol—Gold
6. Sublimatio—Luna—Silver
5. Mortificatio—Mercury—Mercury
4. Conjunctio—Venus—Copper
3. Separatio—Mars—Iron
2. Solutio—Jupiter—Tin
1. Calcinatio—Saturn—Lead
0. Materia Prima—(First Matter)

The standard Renaissance ordering of the alchemical metals, or that is, the standard sequence of laboratory processes, does not correspond with the hierarchical ordering of the seven planets. In other words, The Great Work, or the tranformation of the base metal into gold is not equivalent to the mystical ascent through the seven heavenly spheres found in Gnostic, Jewish (Merkabah/Hekalot), and Sufi mysticism, or the Golden Dawn's aforementioned *Rising on the Planes*.

The transmutation symbolism is not a map for the journey through the planes. This process is a set of keys for gaining access to the Macrocosm. The common aspect of the transmutation symbols is that they all represent a part of the process for abstracting the soul from the body. Though at first glance this appears to be a linear process, it is not. It is an organic process that encourages experimentation. The experiment is to explore various arrangements of the concepts. For many alchemists, pairings of phases are equivalents. For example, Artephius equated Solutio with Coagulatio:

> "But their solution is also their coagulation: They have one and the same operation, for one is not dissolved, but the other is congealed."

Following are descriptions of the Seven Gates, or phases of the transmutation process. For each I have given a description of the laboratory process, some common magical correspondences, common alchemical symbols and emblems, and corresponding mystical concepts. This is not by any stretch a comprehensive catalogue of correspondences, but rather a consolidated distillation of information that might be of use to someone who wants to contemplate the alchemical symbolism towards the goal of achieving the second birth-the Hermetic visionary experience.

Learn about the Seven Gates as they relate to the trance experience, then meditate upon them during the trance state. I recommend that you not use the stages as a rigid step-by-step process. Don't get hung up on any particular order. Experiment. When you use the appropriate key at the right time, the gate will swing open, and you will gain entry to the Macrocosm.

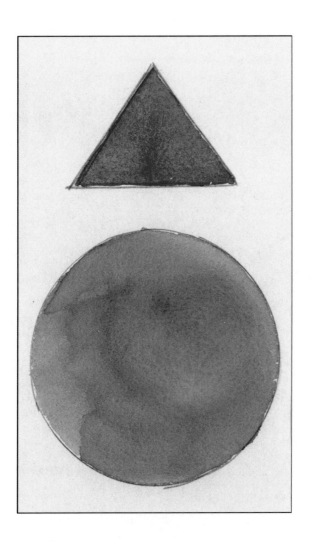

GATE ONE
CALCINATIO

Description of Laboratory Process:
The drying up of humours and matter by fire.

Alchemical Correspondences:
Lead, Saturn

Planetary Angel:
Zaphkiel

Mental Attribute:
Melancholy

Theosophical Attribution:
Sthula Sharira, Elementary Body
Note: I have chosen Franz Hartmann's Theosophical attributions because he spent much of his career studying Paracelsus and Jacob Boehme.

Hitchcock's Interpretation (moral purification):
Both Calcinatio and the following phase, Solutio, are the human conscience.

Hermetic Symbols:
Fire, the starry salamander, The Last Judgement, flaming sword, Hell, the desert, tongues of fire, a sweat-box

Mystical Correspondences:
Calcinatio is the commitment to the journey. Many alchemy texts proclaim that The Great Work begins with prayer and purification of the spirit.

St. Teresa had seven mansions, or stages of mystical process. Her first mansion was prayer.

When Jesus wanted to confront his devil, he went to the desert to fast and meditate. His vision is a classic out of body experience, including a flight to a high vantage point (see the final transmutation phase, Coagulatio).

Due to their mutual emphasis on struggle, purification, and fire, Calcinatio shares commonalities with the Mortificatio phase. One might say that we must descend into the underworld to be baptized by fire in order to attain enlightenment. In this manner, the tarot trump titled The Hanged Man corresponds to this phase. No pain, no gain. If we want to have spiritual experiences, we must do the spiritual work.

Fasting in a desert (asceticism)
Evaporation
Preparation of the will
The beginning of meditation
A primary mortification
Cook the life out of it
Purification (baptism) through fire
Ordeal

GATE TWO
SOLUTIO

Description of Laboratory Process:
The reduction or dissolving of dry matter in a liquid.

Alchemical Correspondences:
Tin, Jupiter

Planetary Angel:
Zadkiel

Mental Attribute:
Ambition and Pride

Theosophical Attribution:
Linga Sharira, The Archaeus (vital force)

Hermetic Symbols:
Water, bathing or drowning King, bathing queen or maiden, bird descending, death and burial, water nymphs, baptism with lunar water, a flood, woman washing clothes, being rained on by heavenly dew,

Hitchcock's Interpretation (moral purification):
Both Solutio and the preceding phase, Calcinatio, are the human conscience.

Mystical Correspondences:
A mystical alchemy interpretation of "Solve et Coagula" (dissolve and coagulate) is to willfully extract the spirit from the body and bring it back with the wisdom of the Macrocosm.

The water of Solutio represents the interconnectedness of the cosmos. To become submerged (baptized) in the water is symbolic of entering the Macrocosm (Astral Plane).

Paracelsus defines a process for connecting with the Macrocosm by referencing the Solutio phase of the alchemical process. Here we find a salient passage where Paracelsus uses alchemical language to refer to the human being, calling us to create a tincture of our body and our imagination.

> "Imagination is the beginning of the growth of a form, and it guides the process of growth. The Will is a dissolving power, which enables the body to become impregnated by the 'tincture' of the imagination. He who wants to know how a man can unite his power of imagination with the power of the imagination of Heaven, must know by what process this may be done. A man comes into possession of creative power by uniting his own mind with the Universal Mind, and he who succeeds in doing so will be in possession of the highest possible wisdom; the lower realm of Nature will be subject to him, and the powers of Heaven will aid him, because Heaven is the servant of wisdom."

Parcelsus is telling us to use our will to dissolve that which obstructs our connection to the Universal Mind (Macrocosmic Intelligence).

One such obstacle is our awareness of our physical body. Dissolve this awareness, and we become a vessel for the Macrocosm. As the Macrocosm pours into our Microcosm, we fall into the inward journey.

GATE THREE
SEPARATIO

Description of Laboratory Process:
The division or separation of bodies.

Alchemical Correspondences:
Iron, Mars

Planetary Angel:
Camael

Mental Attribute:
Fiery Temper

Theosophical Attribution:
Sidereal Body (The Astral Body), Linga Sharira

Hermetic Symbols:
Bird ascending, sword, cutting the philosophical egg, the separation of heaven and earth, Geb lifting Nut above Shu

Mystical Correspondences:
For Paracelsus, separation is the principle of all creation.

The Emerald Tablet reads "Separate the earth from the fire, the subtle from the dense, gently, with great ingenuity." Before we separate our soul from our body, we must learn to make many other separations.

Mars is symbolic of The Will. It is the fiery spirit of war and irascibility, and our ability to separate the necessary from the unnecessary. Particularly important to the practice of meditation is the cultivation of mind control, the ability to silence the incessant mental noise that is a wall between waking consciousness and the mystical state. This is a process of separation via The Will. We must also learn to separate the mind from the body. We must learn to put our body asleep while mind stays awake.

Separatio can also be associated with the dismemberment of the shaman, which happens early in his or her soul journeys. This is a cross-cultural shamanic theme among non-industrial societies, and can also be found in the hermetic literature. Zosimos of Panopolis, an Egyptian alchemist from the late 4th and early 5th centuries, dreamed that a figure named Ion showed him where he had been pierced with a sword, cut to pieces, and burned by fire in order to have his body become spirit. Eliade compared Zosimos' vision to both Dionysius and other gods of the Mysteries, and the initiation visions of shamans. "It is known that every initiation comprises a series of ritual tests symbolizing the death and resurrection of the neophyte."

Writing about the archangel Camael in his book *Theomagia*, John Heydon says

> "He shewes the Natural cause of Wit and Madness, and the nature of Age and Youth; and of the Spirits of the Brain in Sleep and Dreams: For saith he, in Sleep the Spirits of the Brains be still and quiet, but the Soul wanders with me, whilst the parts of the Body all cease at once, and nothing but Air is left to exercise the Organs, if the Meat (to omit the expence of heat) which is continually kept hereby Mars for Health-sake, was neither much, nor of an heavy clogging kind: So neither breathing out foul fapours, nor needing our help to digest it, before we return with the new tidings of secret matters we heard abroad to benefit the body, of secret matters we heard abroad to benefit the body, and then our perceiving Spirits begin to take their places a little before the Mind, and beholds those things we bring home to the Body in particular shapes, which they presently convey to the outside of the body, called the Brain: And this is one cause of Wit."

In the same book, Heydon says that Camael also carries the soul down to the body and raises the dead. These attributes identify Camael as a Mercurial psychopomp, the angel of astral projection.

GATE FOUR
CONJUNCTIO

Description of Laboratory Process:
The combination of elements.

Alchemical Correspondences:
Venus, copper

Planetary Angel:
Haniel

Mental Attribute:
Love and Desire

Theosophical Attribution:
Mumia (Animal Soul), Kama Rupa

Hermetic Symbols:
The great work is the union of opposites--the Sun and the Moon, the King and the Queen, the queen being volatile, and the king being fixed. That which is volatile goes up (spirit) and the earth is fixed.

The Sun and the Moon, The King and the Queen copulating or getting married, their offspring (the Philosophical Child), and their fused self (the Hermaphrodite), dragon killing woman, and woman killing dragon, Yin and Yang (Chinese), Dragon fighting Tiger (Chinese)

Hitchcock's Interpretation (moral purification):
Sol is the human soul, Luna is the human body, and the two are mediated and balanced with what Artephius called Antimonial vinegar, the conscience. Hitchcock called this mediating substance *secret fire*, *hidden fire*, and *invisible fire*, all terms corresponding to the Astral Light.

Corresponding Mystical Concepts:
As above, so below. Solve et Coagula.
Conjunction occurs when two bodies share the same right ascension or ecliptical longitude. The conjunction of sun and moon is an allegory of the marriage of macrocosm and microcrosm by the marriage of the conscious mind with the unconscious mind.

The Secret of the Golden Flower, a Taoist book of mystical alchemy from the 18th century, states: "The heavenly heart lies between the sun and the moon (i.e. the two eyes)." The parenthetical explanation was added by translator Richard Wilhelm, in an addition that included commentary by C. G. Jung. The text goes on:

> "The Book of the Yellow Castle says 'In the square inch of the square foot house, life can be regulated.' The square inch field in the face: What could that be other than the heavenly heart?"

The idea here is that the Yellow Castle, or the heavenly heart, is that which is commonly referred to as the third eye. The Secret of the Golden Flower is a manual for the process of circulating the light, or life energy, through our body, an act which happens through meditation. The heavenly heart, or third eye, is the center of focus, through which all energy flows and is kept in check by the meditator.

Between the sun (conscious mind) and the moon (unconscious mind), resides the Yellow Castle (psychic center).

As Paracelsus offered in this veiled riddle:

> "The knowledge of Nature as it is--not as we imagine it to be--constitutes true philosophy. He who merely sees the external appearance of things is not a philosopher; the true philosopher sees the reality, not merely the outward appearance. He who knows the sun and the moon has a sun and a moon in him, and he can tell how they look, even if his eyes are shut. Thus the true physician sees in himself the whole constitution of the Microcosm of man, with all its parts."

One curious image from The Comte de St. Germain's *The Most Holy Trinosophia* (late 18th century) reveals trance's role in Western alchemy. The drawing shows the alchemist gazing intently into a circular dish. He is scrying, and superimposed over the pedestal holding his dish is an image of the conjunction of the sun and the moon. I have quoted a passage detailing one of the author's visions in the next gate, Mortificatio.

GATE FIVE
MORTIFICATIO

Description of Laboratory Process:
Three specific phases: Nigredo (black), Albedo (white), Rubedo (red)

Alchemical Correspondences:
Mercury, Mercury

Planetary Angel:
Michael

Mental Attribute:
Intelligence

Theosophical Attribution:
The Rational Soul (Human Soul), Flesh of Adam—Manas

Hermetic Symbols:
Sword, death, murder, mutilation, torture, skeleton, crow or raven, Sol and Luna slaying the dragon

Hitchcock's Interpretation (moral purification):
Hitchcock interpreted mortificatio to be humility. He thought of albedo as a symbol of purity.

Corresponding Mystical Concepts:
The soul and spirit are trapped in the body. The body must be mortified in order to release the soul and spirit.

Although Plotinus, in his letter to Flaccus, stated that there are "different roads" for achieving ecstasy, he does mention one method in particular:

> "Purify your soul from all undue hope and fear about earthly things, mortify the body, deny self—affections as well as appetites—and the inner eye will begin to exercise its clear and solemn vision."

Spirit guides are often mentioned in alchemical texts. In Book V of The Comte De St. Germaine's *The Most Holy Trinosophia*,

"I had been lifted to a tremendous height. My invisible guide left me and I descended again. For quite a long time I rolled through space; already the earth spread out before my confused vision… I could estimate how many minutes would pass until I would be crushed on the rocks. But quick as thought my guide darts down beside me, takes hold of me, lifts me up again, and again lets me fall. Finally he raises me with him to an immeasurable distance. I saw globes revolve around me and earths gravitate at my feet. Suddenly the genius who bore me touched my eyes and I swooned."

St. Teresa's fifth mansion is characterized as a "prayer of union", and is visualized as a cocoon that enshrouds the body.

Teresa, in her description of this vision, wrote that an angel had a spear with a flame at its tip, and it stabbed her with the spear repeatedly, jerking out her entrails with a pain so great that it made her moan. As mentioned in GATE THREE: SEPARATIO, a cross-cultural examination reveals that a common trope in the experience of the trancer is that of having his or her body torn apart and reassembled. Though this relates to Separatio, it is best likened to Mortifactio, the death phase. It's also referred to as the torment of the metals.

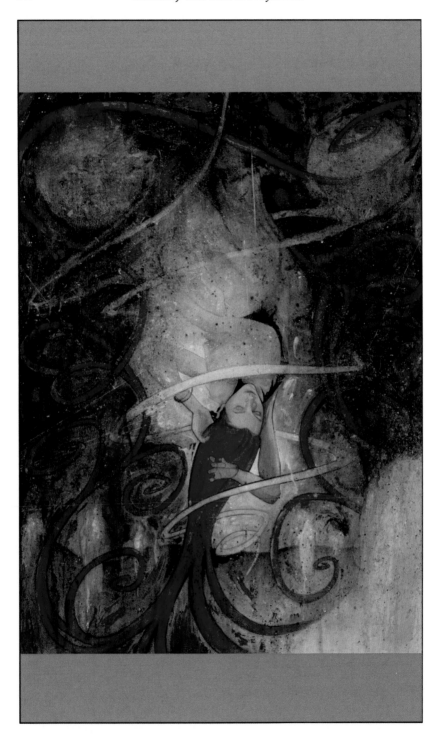

GATE SIX
SUBLIMATIO

Description of Laboratory Process:
Elevation of the matter to a spiritual state.

Alchemical Correspondences:
Luna, Silver

Planetary Angel:
Gabriel

Mental Attribute:
Dreamy disposition

Theosophical Attribution:
The Spiritual Soul, Buddhi—Flesh of Christ

Hermetic Symbols:
Air, the ascent, white bird ascending, assumption, the Rapture, a ladder, the tower of Babel

Corresponding Mystical Concepts:
Sublimatio is the transmutation phase that can be most directly related to astral projection. It is the phase whereby the alchemist extracts the spirit from the body.

It is in her sixth mansion that St. Teresa describes ecstasy.

> "There is another form of rapture, which, though essentially the same as the last, yet produces very different feelings in the soul. I call it the 'flight of the spirit,' 1 for the soul suddenly feels so rapid a sense of motion that the spirit appears to hurry it away with a speed which is very alarming, especially at first."

And later, she states:

> "To return to this sudden rapture of the spirit. The soul really appears to have quitted the body, which however is not lifeless, and though, on the other hand, the person is certainly not dead,

yet she herself cannot, for a few seconds, tell whether her spirit remains within her body or not. 9 She feels that she has been wholly transported into another and a very different region from that in which we live, where a light so unearthly is shown 10 that, if during her whole lifetime she had been trying to picture it and the wonders seen, she could not possibly have succeeded. In an instant her mind learns so many things at once that if the imagination and intellect spent years in striving to enumerate them, it could not recall a thousandth part of them. This vision is not intellectual but imaginary and is seen by the eyes of the soul more clearly than earthly things are seen by our bodily eyes. Although no words are pronounced, the spirit is taught many truths; for instance, if it beholds any of the saints, it knows them at once as well as if intimately acquainted with them for years."

GATE SEVEN
COAGULATIO

Description of Laboratory Process:
Coagulatio is the final phase, the changing of the substance back to solid state. It's a return of spirit to the matter that houses it, whose return results in the purification of the material self.

Alchemical Correspondences:
Sun, Gold

Planetary Angel:
Raphael

Mental Attribute:
Wisdom

Theosophical Attribution:
The Man of the New Olympus, Atma Buddhi Manas

Hermetic Symbols:
Eagle chained to a ground animal, post-Flood, the stone of Saturn, sewing seeds, eating food, the magus and his psychopomp on a mountain.

Corresponding Mystical Concepts:
In mystical terms, Coagulatio is the culmination of The Great Work. It is attainment, the mastery of self, the confirmation of expanded reality via a profound journey to the Macrocosm. From a Jungian perspective, it is the assimilation of the mystical experience within our self-understanding.

BOOK III

OCCULT PNEUMATOLOGY

OCCULT PNEUMATOLOGY

Pneumatology is defined by Webster's Dictionary as "the study of spirit beings or phenomena". According to Franz Hartmann, it's the study of semi-material spirits, as "pneuma" means "soul", not "spirit".

An important thing to note about Renaissance Hermetic philosophy and spiritualism is that communication with the dead was not a commonly held belief. Paracelsus says the sidereal bodies (souls) of the deceased can't be conjured, because they have no sense. Instead, when they are conjured, devils (elementals) take possession of the sidereal bodies and play pranks with the conjurers.

Below is a list of the semi-material entities that exist on the astral plane, as discussed by Paracelsus in the Renaissance, and by the Theosophists in the late 19th century.

Athnici
Elemental fire spirits. Balls of fire or orbs of light, as witnessed during séances.

Aquastor (Tulpa)
An entity created by the human imagination. Such beings include Elementals, Succubi, Incubi, and Vampires. They draw upon the life of the person who created them, or attach themselves to another person to draw upon their life force.

Astral Body (Sidereal Body)
The form of a person, or any other living entity, caused by thought or the will of the imagination.

Cabali,Cables,Lemures
The earthbound ghosts of people who died a premature death.

Durdales (Dryades)
Semi-material Elemental spirits that live in the trees.

Elementals
Elementals are nature spirits that exist on the Elemental Plane. As the Astral Plane exists above the frequency of the Material Plane, The El-

ementary Plane exists below the frequency of the Material Plane. Elementals may be glimpsed during waking consciousness.

Elementaries
The astral corpses of the dead. The spirit has departed, but the mind lives on.

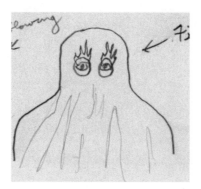

Evestrum
A person's Thought Body. It guards over us by paying attention to knowledge through its connection with the Macrocosm. The more we sleep and meditate, the more active our Evestrum becomes. It reveals information to us through images.

Flagae
Familiar Spirits. They tend to communicate through a mirror or beryllus.

Gigantes (Giants)
Enormous, humanoid elementals. They live as we do, though are rarely glimpsed, as they live on their plane.

Gnomi, Pymaei, Cabitali
An Earth Elemental. Small humanoids living in the earth. Known to be hard workers, they work the energies of the earth. Wood nymphs. Different species have been distinguished. Some say the Pygmaei (Dwarves) are continuously at war with the Gnomi.

Homunculi
A human created by an alchemist or magician without being gestated in a female womb. One recipe is to incubate sperm in horse dung for 40 days. This is black magic.

Homunculi Imagunculae
Images made of clay, wax, wood, etc, to stimulate the imagination in the production of a Tulpa, typically for the purpose of harming or aiding another person. This is black magic.

Incubus
A male parasite unintentionally created by lust.

Lemures
Air Elementals, or an Elementary component of the dead, that manifests itself physically, usually during Spritualist activities, such as a séance.

Melosinae (also Undines)
Water Elementals. Mermaids. Water nymphs. They are humanoid, but may also appear as fish or snakes.

Nenufareni (also Sylphs)
Air Elementals. Fairies. Humanoid in form.

Nymphae
Elementals of water plants.

Pennates, Lares, Hercii, Etesii, Meilichii
Fire Spirits. Hobgoblins. Attached to places, such as haunted houses.
Produce physical phenomena, such as noises, object throwing, etc.

Phantasmata
Entities created by the imaginations of people. They might communicate with their creator.

Rupa
Form. The Kama-rupa is a form caused by desire. The Mayavi-rupa is a
form caused by the will of the imagination.

Sagani
Another term for Earth Elementals.

Salamanders
Fire Elementals.

Sylphes (Not to be confused with Sylphs)
Elementals that live in the mountains.

Succubus
A female parasite unintentionally created by lust.

Thoughtform
Thought, whether consciously or unconsciously,
materialized into form.

Trarames
A counterpart to the Evestrum, it's an invisible, attendant power that communicates with humans through sound, such as astral bells, voices, etc.

Tulpas
See Aquastor.

Umbratiles
Shadows becoming tangible through life force borrowed from a medium. Doppelganger, wraith, Scin-lecca. Like the Evestrum, if it doesn't return the life force to its host, the host risks death.

Vampires
Astral parasites. See Incubus, Succubus, and Aquastor (Tulpa). Astral bodies of the living or the dead can also be vampires.

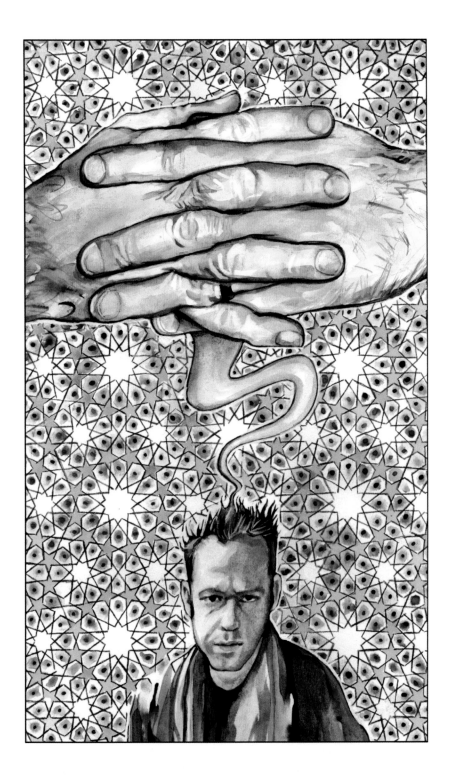

APPENDICES

THE EMERALD TABLET

1.   Tis true without lying, certain & most true.

2.   That which is below is like that which is above & that which is above is like that which is below to do the miracles of one only thing

3.   And as all things have been & arose from one by the mediation of one: so all things have their birth from this one thing by ad aptation.

4.   The Sun is its father, the moon its mother, the wind hath car ried it in its belly, the earth is its nurse.

5.   The father of all perfection in the whole world is here.

6.   Its force or power is entire if it be converted into earth.

7.   Separate thou the earth from the fire, the subtile from the gross sweetly with great indoustry.

8.   It ascends from the earth to the heaven & again it descends to the earth & receives the force of things superior & inferior.

9.   By this means you shall have the glory of the whole world

10.   & thereby all obscurity shall fly from you.

11.   Its force is above all force. For it vanquishes every subtile thing & penetrates every solid thing.

12.   So was the world created.

13.   From this are & do come admirable adaptations whereof the means (or process) is here in this. Hence I am called Hermes Trismegist, having the three parts of the philosophy of the whole world

14.   That which I have said of the operation of the Sun is accomplished & ended.

Translated by Isaac Newton

FURTHER READING

Though the astral projection phenomenon, under the guise of many terms, has been written about for more than 2,000 years, attempts to explain it in detailed, straightforward language are limited to the modern era, spanning little more than the past century. Because of this, and because academic circles have just recently shown an interest in esoteric studies, we've yet to see very much writing at all that draws comparisons between astral projection and other bodies of knowledge.

In the late 19th and early 20th centuries, several members of the Theosophical Society wrote about the astral body and astral projection. Their theories are derived from Hindu and Buddhist beliefs. A notable example is Charles Leadbeater's *The Astral Plane, its scenery, inhabitants, and phenomena* (1895). One Theosophist, Oliver Fox, wrote practical advice on the subject. His articles "The Pineal Doorway" and "Beyond the Pineal Door" appeared in issue 31 of the journal Occult Review (1920). These articles were influential to the first practical handbook on astral projection, Sylvan Muldoon and Herewood Carrington's *Projection of The Astral Body*, published in 1929. Though influenced by Fox, Muldoon and Carrington were not Theosophists, but rather belonged to Spiritualism, the tradition that brought us the séances and psychic mediumship so popular in the nineteenth century. In 1939, Fox's book *Astral Projection: A Record of Research* was published. Subsequent editions of his book are subtitled "A Record of Out-of-the-Body Experiences". In his Foreword for editions of this book published by University Books, John C. Wilson notes that Fox never wrote the term "Astral Projection". He theorizes that it was the popularity of Muldoon and Carrington's book that caused publishers to superimpose this term upon Fox's work, for marketing purposes. Wilson stated that "Astral Projection" is an inadequate term, because, according to Theosophical doctrine, the astral body was just one of five bodies, "and not at all the most spiritual". But, as Wilson wrote, "Astral Projection" is the term "most familiar to people today, and one will have to be content with it."

It was the 1971 publication of Robert Monroe's *Journeys Beyond the Body*, and his founding of The Monroe Institute the following year, that really fostered contemporary interest in the subject. Although the phrase "out-of-the-body" first appeared in the title of the second edition of Oliver Fox's book, Monroe popularized the term. He shortened the term to "out of body" and its abbreviation "OBE" shifting the language away from the mystical and superstitious sounding term "astral projection" to give the phenomenon a more clinical sound, thereby making it more palatable for a broader community. Monroe, who had a career in radio, was trying to develop technology that would help people learn information during sleep when he accidentally induced his own initial OBEs.

The 1970s saw a surge of interest in related phenomena. In 1975, Raymond Moody's *Life After Life*, a book on NDEs was published. Also notable for generating contemporary excitement is the laboratory research of Dr. Stanislav Grof, Dr. Charles Tart, and Dr. Stephen LaBerge, respectively, and the practical, nuts-and-bolts processes of writers such as Robert Bruce and William Buhlman. I highly recommend Bruce's book *Astral Dynamics*.

The narrative constructed in the preceding paragraphs is by no means a comprehensive history of modern literature on astral projection. There are less known, yet notable books on the subject, such as Ophiel's *The Art and Practice of Astral Projection* and J. H. Brennan's *Astral Doorways* (two of my favorite books), and the works of Yram, Robert Crookall, and others. At this point, the literature is largely an underground, non-mainstream body of knowledge.

The one significant book that investigates astral projection in the context of another field of study is Mircea Eliade's highly esteemed *Shamanism: Archaic Techniques of Ecstasy* (1951), which focuses specifically on the history of shamanism and spirit travel. Eliade also wrote a book on alchemy, *The Forge and the Crucible* (1956), in which he said little about the spirit travel of the alchemist, and was in fact rather dismissive about the whole issue. For Eliade, any experience the alchemists had couldn't have possibly been parallel to the experience of the non-industrial shaman.

In the late 19th century, Franz Hartmann excavated information that sheds considerable light on the relationship between Renaissance alchemy and astral projection, though exploring these connections was not his priority. Perhaps the timing wasn't right. Still, this treatise owes more debt to Hartmann than any other writer. At The Lloyd Library, I discovered Hartmann's *Paracelsus: Life and Teachings*, and was astounded by the wealth of information Hartmann amassed on the magical philosophies of Paracelsus. Hartmann was a Theosophist, and when reading his book, one must be careful to discern between his beliefs and those of Paracelsus. Still, his work is a treasure trove of information, as he sought out and interpreted into English many of Paracelsus' long forgotten and disregarded writings. Hartmann also wrote Magic Black and White, in which he continues to discuss related topics.

In the Lloyd Library's archives, I was further delighted to discover the correspondence between Hartmann and John Uri Lloyd. It turns out that Hartmann translated the German edition of *Etidorhpa* (German edition 1897). Though a work of fiction, *Etidorhpa* has its own significance in the alchemical tradition, and in fact, touches upon the relationship between alchemy and spirit travel, as can be seen in the quote at the beginning of my Acknowledgments, and in the illustration (reprinted here on page 28) of the psychopomp touring a soul about the Macrocosmic Astral Plane.

TRANCE INDUCTION

The space between the sun and the moon is the trance state, a condition of equilibrium in which the conscious and unconscious minds work in conjunction. This is a prolonged hypnagogic or hypnopompic state that is the product of the mystical practitioner who has mastered the art of mind control.

If you learn to sustain consciousness during the hypnagogic and hypnopompic states, the gates will open, and you will experience the Macrocosm.

Master the art of mind control. Meditate. Pay attention. Keep a dream journal.

In thee is hid the Treasure of Treasures.

KNOW THYSELF.

Made in the USA
Monee, IL
01 June 2021